There Must Be Elephants in Heaven

Cynthia Zaragoza

Illustrations by Charles Clark

WestBow Press books may be ordered through booksellers or by contacting:

WestBow Press
A Division of Thomas Nelson
1663 Liberty Drive
Bloomington, IN 47403
www.westbowpress.com
1-(866) 928-1240

ISBN: 978-1-4497-7938-2 (sc)
ISBN: 978-1-4497-7939-9 (e)

Library of Congress Control Number: 2012923539

Printed in the United States of America

WestBow Press rev. date: 1/10/2013

WestBow
PRESS
A DIVISION OF THOMAS NELSON

Little Danny arrived at his Grandma's house with his favorite stuffed elephant in his arms.

He climbed up onto her lap then said, “Grandma Baby Ricky is sick. He’s going to go to heaven.”

With a tender touch and gentle voice Grandma said, “Yes. Your baby brother is going to go to heaven. But, you know the bible says that the lion and the lamb will lay down together as friends. So if there is a lion and there is a lamb, then there must be elephants in heaven too.”

“Do you really think there are elephants there?” Little Danny squealed with excitement.

“Well God said that the animals will live in peace with one another and that they will not fight or even think about eating each other up. Even the wolf will be happy to live with the lamb.

There must be elephants in heaven.

The leopard, after a long day of running with the cheetah and going for a swim with the hippos, will choose to lay right down by the goat.

There must be elephants in heaven.

In heaven Baby Ricky might decide to take a walk
down the streets of gold with some of his friends.
The young cow, the big lion, and a little shaggy dog.
So I really do believe there are elephants in heaven!

If a very very hungry lion would see Ricky walking by, he wouldnt choose him for supper. He would go join the ox in eating some delicious golden straw.

So there must be elephants in heaven.

It will be funny to see the cow and bear near a bush eating some juicy red berries together.

Elephants? Yes, I really do believe they will be there.

Ricky might see the hole of a snake and be curious to find his slithering little friend. He will reach into the snake's comfy little home and the snake will not bite him.

If there is a snake, then there must be elephants in heaven.

Well what do you know about that! There are elephants in heaven.

In heaven there is the Crystal Sea, and elephants love the water. I can just imagine Baby Ricky jumping on the back of a baby elephant and guiding him to the water's edge. With a giggle and a laugh, Baby Ricky will tell his friend to suck water up into his trunk.

As Gabriel, the archangel, gives his great big daddy elephant a nice cool drink of the sweet tasty waters,

Baby Ricky will whisper to his little floppy eared friend to squirt the majestic angel right in the face!

Imagine the look of surprise on Gabriel's face as the crystal sea water hangs from his nose and chin!

But when he sees the joy and excitement on the face of Baby Ricky and his little friend, he can't help but let out a roar of laughter that touches the heart of every angel in heaven.

"Danny, there are a lot of wonderful things in heaven.

Baby Ricky will have so much fun there with the playful wolf,

the fluffy lamb,

spotted leopard,

bearded goat,

mooing cow,

magnificent lion,

yipping dog,

cuddly bear,

strong ox,

slithering snake,

oh yes... and his baby elephant!"

CPSIA information can be obtained
at www.ICGtesting.com
Printed in the USA
LVIC052335140313
324383LV00001B
* 9 7 8 1 4 4 9 7 7 9 3 8 2 *